STRONG TOWERS

MEN'S DEVOTIONAL:

7 WEEKS OF CHALLENGE AND WISDOM

Strong Towers
35109 Harry Byrd Hwy
Round Hill, VA 20151
www.strong-towers.com

This book is the work of a group of nine men who have committed to growing in Christ together: Zach Detweiler, Tom Edwards, TJ Bramblett, Shawn Ludeker, Michael Lara, Michael Haynes, Jon Ackerman, Alex Voorhees, and Alex James. It could not have been made with out each of those men and their commitment to one another.

PROLOGUE

Welcome, friends! This devotional grew out of the collected wisdom of a group of nine men. It began as a way to challenge and encourage one another to become the men and leaders God has designed them to be. You get to be the 10th man in the group! You can join us as we share with us as we challenge each other and share the wisdom we have found to build each other up and become strong.

Use this devotional to dig deeper into scripture, dig deeper into the wisdom of those who have come before you, and dig deeper into your relationship with the Father. Use this devotional to strengthen your relationships with other like-minded men. We are not meant to battle alone.

God has called you to a specific role in the Kingdom. We believe that your time on this Earth is meant to grow and shape you for that role. We believe God has called you to rule over part of his Kingdom here on Earth as part of your preparation for the life to come. This book is meant to spur that process.

As you read through the devotional, you will see that we believe God has things to say to you. We will talk about the things God has told us. If you are not familiar with this, one of the easiest ways to start hearing God speak is to sit silently and ask him a question from the end of one of the daily entries. Something like, "God, do I favor maintaining my spiritual work more than the innovation of breakthrough?" Then, sit and listen. With practice, you will learn to discern the voice of our Father from your own voice and the voice of the enemy. We also recommend writing down what you hear because it is easy to forget what God has told you. For a deeper study of this topic, we highly recommend *A Guide for Listening and Inner Healing Prayer* by Rusty Rustenbach.

The entries in this devotional are written by different members of our men's group because we believe the whole is greater than the sum of the parts. As it says in 1 Corinthians 12:12 NLT, "The human body has many parts, but the many parts make up one whole body. So it is with the body of Christ." We have taken the perspective in this book that the knowledge and wisdom of the group is greater than that of any one person.

We arranged the book into weekly chapters. Each week there are five shorter words of wisdom or challenge and one deep dive. Please reflect on the daily reading and let it stir inside of you. There are many ways to engage with the content in this book. We suggest starting with a short prayer and then read through the devotional and any scriptures referenced. Lastly, you should take some time to reflect on the devotional and write down your reactions, thoughts, or what God has told you.

Why 7 weeks? We wanted to create something that could help challenge you in your walk with God on a daily basis. We wanted it to be long enough to create a habit but not so long that it seemed like a daunting commitment. It makes the experience achievable, repeatable, and shareable.

While you can do this devotional by yourself, we are not meant to fight alone. Find like-minded men who are seeking growth like you. Share your responses with them. Create a group text discussion or get together on Saturday mornings. Our prayer for this devotional is that it will play a part in helping your group build up and become strong.

MAINTENANCE VS INNOVATION

I listened to an author who just wrote a book that lays out how our society is too focused on **innovation** and not enough on **maintenance**.[1] For example, I remember when upgrading parts on a computer to keep in running was the best option, but now it is easier to just buy a new one.

This made me think about some things in my life and made me curious how much this extended to my spiritual life. Examples of maintenance could be growing my faith in the Father by reading the Bible, praying, and worshiping. Innovation could be miraculous signs, God speaking, and manifesting the gifts of the Spirit. Do I favor maintenance or innovation? Am I drawn to one and ignore the other? How can I balance both?

DO I FAVOR MAINTENANCE OR INNOVATION?

[1] The Art of Manliness Podcast #658: In Praise of Maintenance in a World Obsessed With Innovation, https://www.artofmanliness.com/articles/podcast-658-in-praise-of-maintenance-in-a-world-obsessed-with-innovation/

WEEK 1.DAY 2
DO YOU PRACTICE WHAT YOU PREACH?

"Even though I've spent thirty years as a counselor teaching other people how to be gracious to their souls, I've always been rather hard on my own." John Eldredge

This quotation pulled me up short this morning. It feels like challenge and strangely, at the same time, relief.

I respect John enough to want to pursue something that he values, but his admission that he hasn't arrived yet also takes off some of the pressure that I put on myself to get it all right, right now.

WHAT HAVE YOU BEEN TEACHING BUT STILL NEED TO LEARN?

WEEK 1.DAY 3
PRESS ON TOWARD THE GOAL

My encouragement for you today is from Philippians.

"Brothers, I do not consider that I have made it my own. But one thing I do: forgetting what lies behind and straining forward to what lies ahead, I press on toward the goal for the prize of the upward call of God in Christ Jesus." Philippians 3:13-14 ESV

Do you feel like you need to *press on toward the goal* in the face of opposition. God has also encouraged me to think about pressing forward in the right way, framed by these two verses:

"...I have learned the secret of facing plenty and hunger, abundance and need. I can do all things through him who strengthens me." Philippians 4:12-13 ESV

"Let us therefore strive to enter that rest..." Hebrews 4:11 ESV

WHERE DO YOU NEED TO PRESS ON TOWARD THE PRIZE?

WEEK 1.DAY 4
HAVE FAITH

My reading from scripture this morning couldn't have been more timely in the midst of the coronavirus pandemic. I'm reminded that I stand in his grace daily; not for a second, a minute, an hour, a month, even a year, but eternally and in that I have hope for the future he is shaping for us.

"Therefore, since we have been justified by faith, we have peace with God through our Lord Jesus Christ. Through him we have also obtained access by faith into this grace in which we stand, and we rejoice in hope of the glory of God. Not only that, but we rejoice in our sufferings, knowing that suffering produces endurance, and endurance produces character, and character produces hope, and hope does not put us to shame, because God's love has been poured into our hearts through the Holy Spirit who has been given to us." Romans 5:1-5 ESV

I often view suffering as punishment, but God clearly lays out how these are tools of growth. I have found this is a hard message when you are in the suffering so I study these scriptures before the suffering. Then, they are stored in my heart, and I can turn to them in the midst of the pain.

WHEN HAVE YOU PERSEVERED THROUGH PAIN AND WHAT HOPE DID THAT BRING?

WEEK 1.DAY 5
YOU ARE A MASTERPIECE

Watching church from home a couple of weeks ago with my boys, I found myself admiring my sons and how intently they were listening—a rarity in my home. All of a sudden they both leaped up at the start of the music.♪♫ "For we are God's masterpiece. He has created us anew in Christ Jesus, so we can do the good things he planned for us long ago."
Ephesians 2:10 NLT♪♫

I laughed and smiled thinking to myself what a joy to learn that at such a young age. My older son grabbed my hand and nodding his head to beat, while pointing at me he sang "♪♫we are God's masterpiece♪♫ that means you too, Dad, so dance!"

I struggle with fear, the fear of not living up to my potential or the image of the perfect dad I have created in my mind. But listening to my boys sing to our Father, a song of pure joy of being his masterpiece, reminded me that God created me to be the man I am now as well as the man I will become.

I've been raving about Steven Pressfield's *The War of Art* and one chapter reminded me of being fearfully and wonderfully made and how much I want to be the man God has created me to be and not the person "I" have imagined.

WHO HAS GOD CREATED YOU TO BE?

HOW ARE YOU LIVING THAT OUT TODAY?

DEEP DIVE: TREAT YOURSELF TO THE REAL WORLD

I woke up yesterday on the second day of the year and prepared to go for a run, since I had resolved to start exercising again. The outside temperature was 32 degrees, almost enough to convince me to stay inside. However, last night I heard a guy talking about how we live in an artificial world and seldom interact with things in their natural state. Think about it: you wake up in your 72-degree bedroom, drive your toasty car to work, sit in your climate-controlled office, maybe go lift some weights at the gym or run on a treadmill, and then return to your warm home. Not only do I seldom spend time in the real climate, but also on a normal day my feet don't even touch dirt. I walk on carpet, wood flooring, concrete, or asphalt all day long.

WE LIVE IN AN ARTIFICIAL WORLD AND SELDOM INTERACT WITH THINGS IN THEIR NATURAL STATE.

This is rough on my soul. I have a friend who likes to cycle, and we were talking about indoor cycling trainers. You know how we described riding one of those for two hours? Soul crushing. However, a two hour ride on country roads would be life-giving. Would you rather go for a two hour hike or walk on an inclined treadmill for two hours?

THE CRAZY BUSY LIVES WE LIVE IN THIS ARTIFICIAL WORLD ARE MAKING OUR SOULS MORE SHALLOW.

I have started digging into some teaching on rest, restoration, and taking care of your soul, and many of these teachers talk about how hurried, hectic, distracted, and fractured our lives are. I started contemplating what gives my soul rest and when does my soul feel most connected to the Father. For me, getting into nature helps shut down my mind and lets my soul breath.

The realization of all this teaching was enough to get me out the door and into the frosty day. I didn't turn on a podcast or music but instead just ran. My heart and soul were crying out for something real. I felt the cold air in my lungs and the pavement under my feet. Wait, pavement, ugh, that's not natural. Then 1.5 miles into my run, there was a trailhead for mountain bike trails. My mind said "stay on the paved path because you could hold a faster pace on the smooth flat surface." But my soul said, "I need some of the real world." So I took a right turn onto the mountain bike trails and my soul rejoiced. The uneven terrain, the frost on the branches, the deer jumping up and running—these were real.

THE FATHER WAS SAYING, "WELCOME TO MY CREATION."

As I continued, I kept seeing places that looked great to sit: a large rock by a stream or a log at just the right height. So I paused and sat. I took long and deep breaths and soaked in the real world. The deer on the hill, the sun rising in the east, the sound of a stream. It was refreshing; no, it was **restoring** me to the life that was all around. It wasn't my kids fighting, the GIFs in a group text, or deadlines at work fast approaching. It was creation; it was real.

I felt the Father saying to me, "This is what I have for you in they year. Rest in me, and I will restore you. I will settle your soul. Just rest in me and pursue me. Come find me here in the real world. Your hands might get cold. You might twist your ankle on the trail. It might rain. But those are the moments when I will give you what you need."

WE NEED TO LISTEN TO OUR SOUL WHEN IT IS CRYING OUT FOR A QUIET WALK BY A STREAM.

It is crazy to think that I am just realizing the effect that being out in nature has on my soul. Last year, I was training for a 100-mile race, so I did two long runs every weekend from December through April. I couldn't skip the runs because I knew I needed the training to survive the 100 miles in April. I had to run in the rain and snow. Looking back, I recognize how my soul felt alive in those times. The conversations with my training partners were about deep topics as we slogged out the miles in the 4 AM rain. But after the race, I retreated to the artificial world. Back to treadmills and gym workouts.

FOR MOST OF US, THE REAL WORLD HAS BEEN REPLACED BY AN ARTIFICIAL AND DIGITAL WORLD.

Our idea of resting is binge-watching Netflix. We need to think about what this does to our souls. Have you ever finished watching a series and said, "Ah, I feel so restored, like I have been with the Father."

Are we losing our ability to have deep conversations and connections because our souls are becoming more shallow? Did you even have the attention span to make it here to the fourth page entry? We need to listen to our soul when it is crying out for a quiet walk by a stream. I know it is something I am working on one cold run at a time.

WEEK 2.DAY 1
BEER VS JESUS

I heard someone speak on fasting, and it reminded me of an old podcast[2] that discussed what we put in front of God. Here is the test: ask yourself what could I give up for 30 days and note how your inner man responds.

For me, it was surprising how hard it was to give up beer. Now, this was not about will power. The purpose of the exercise is to learn where you are seeking comfort from created things. Instead, we should be seeking comfort from the Father. So make sure you don't fulfill the beer craving with ice cream (that's what I did the first week).

Once you find the thing you are holding onto and need to fast from, here is a prayer to pray:

Jesus, there are places in my heart that I much prefer to entrust to the immediate comfort of (insert your thing here: beer, podcasts, TV, food, sex, work, sugar, coffee, sarcasm, etc) more than I desire you. I bring the truth of who I am to the truth of who you are, and I receive your love for me right here.

WHERE ARE YOU SEEKING COMFORT?

---

[2]https://www.becomegoodsoil.com/2013/04/24/i-love-beer-more-than-jesus/
https://www.becomegoodsoil.com/podcast/026-for-all-who-are-thirsty-podcast/

SUBURBAN VS FRONTIER

One of my all-time favorite quotes on the topic of living a deeply rewarding spiritual life is this one from Howard Macy.

"The spiritual life cannot be made suburban. It is always frontier and we who live in it must accept and even rejoice that it remains untamed." Howard Macy

What are your frontiers? The places you feel inexperienced and ill-equipped, but where you also feel God's invitation to brave discomfort to uncover something new and good.

WHAT ARE YOUR FRONTIERS?

WEEK 2.DAY 3
BEING INEFFICIENT

A couple weeks ago I was struggling with one of my deeper wounds -- the "it's all up to me" one. I was in a spiral of feeling like "everyone else" needed my help with their stuff but no one was able or willing to help me with mine, and so I always have to pull double-duty.

It was also hitting on my "unforgivable sin"...the thing I most struggle with in others: Don't be needy! Take care of your own stuff! Don't need help!

As I was looking out the kitchen window into our backyard and wrestling with these tensions, God dropped a very disruptive question: "Would you want to not be needed? Would you want to not be necessary?"

Dang! No!

The fog started to lift a little with that question, but I could still feel my flesh insisting that things at least be "more balanced." As I fought with that, I realized "more balanced" really just meant "I do my things and they do their things"...a default to efficiency and self-sufficiency I've had my whole life.

God very kindly pointed out that's not the way he handles much of anything. In fact, the more he helped me understand, the more I saw just how wildly inefficient he is.

He has all the power to do what needs to be done and all the wisdom to do it correctly. And yet he *insists* on doing the work with us...which means it takes 1000x longer and results in infinitely more mistakes and disruptions.

And he does it because it's better that way.

Because it involves love...and discovery...and partnership.

And so I repent again for choosing the less-good thing. For prioritizing efficiency over love. For being frustrated with others who invite inefficiency by prioritizing togetherness and shared experience.

LORD, HELP ME CHOOSE THE BETTER THINGS TODAY.

WEEK 2.DAY 4
INTUITION VS INTELLECT

For a while now, I've been quietly wrestling with the possibility of this "life through the lens of the gospel" thing being labeled as merely an intellectual exercise—a sort of theological brainstorming in order to feel one's way through life. It doesn't feel like a purely intellectual process, but it's not exactly direct, explicit conversation with God either.

The book I'm currently crawling through is the classic *Becoming Who You Are* by Dutch Sheets. And what he says about the spirit has been helpful for me:

"Our spirit is the part of us that God intended to connect with or relate to him; not only him but also the entire spiritual realm. It shouldn't be surprising then, to know it houses our conscience and intuition."

"The spirit of man is the lamp of the Lord, searching all his innermost parts." Proverbs 20:27 ESV

I just want to encourage you to dig deeper than your intellect this week. There is a divine intuition within us eager to guide us according to what we know to be true in the gospel, and it's way better, faster, and more accurate than our intellect.

DO YOU DEPEND ON YOUR INTELLECT OR INTUITION?

SUPERNATURAL

"No Buddhist claims a supernatural life but frequently lives a more consistent one than Christians. How often the so-called Christian, even while proclaiming some of the loftiest truths one could ever express, lives a life bereft of that beauty and character." Ravi Zacharias, *The Logic of God: 52 Christian Essentials for the Heart and Mind*

Many religions don't have a supernatural component, but ours does, and so our faith ought to look that way. If you have a hard time expressing that, take a moment to reflect if you truly believe all of what the gospels say.

If we did believe it completely, the very nature of those truths would change how we go about **everything** in our lives. I've realized that there are still areas of my faith where my belief is weak - it may be stronger than any other belief I have, but there are many areas of my life where the gospels have not influenced my life to the extent I would expect them to.

INSTEAD OF "TRYING TO BELIEVE HARDER" PRAY EACH MORNING FOR A GREATER REVELATION OF THE GOSPELS.

DEEP DIVE: REST

"BUSY IS THE NEW STUPID." -BILL GATES

In the last few months, my friends and I have started discussing this concept of the busy, hurried, meeting-packed, over-committed, hectic lives we live. We have come across multiple resources (podcasts, sermons, books, apps) talking about rest, sabbath, soul-care, self-care, eliminating hurry, or some other way to describe the cure for the problem of the crazy pace of life that plagues us all.

WE HAVE BOUGHT INTO THE LIE THAT TECHNOLOGY WILL MAKE US MORE EFFICIENT AND MAKE OUR LIVES EASIER.

We are busy, frantic, and hurried as we hustle around our daily lives. While technology has removed much of the manual labor, it has also removed us from many of the natural rhythms of life that we were intended to experience.

Think about this: until the invention of trains in the 1800s, typical humans travelled at 3 miles per hour walking or 4 miles per hour on a horse. To have a relationship with someone, you had to walk or ride to go see them. Now, we can commute 45 miles like it is nothing and have "friends" that you have never met in person, all while not even knowing your neighbors.

We are addicted to the speed and hurry. We like it. I realized I really like speed, hustle, and hurry while listening to the *Fight Hustle, End Hurry Podcast* by John Mark Comer and Jefferson Bethke. From my time in the military, I learned that I perform well in a crisis. I have brought this into my work and family life. While there is part of this that is God-given, there is also a large part of this that is my attempt to run from the pain of this life. When they made this point, it really hit home for me. The hustle and hurry in my life has stopped me from examining myself.

WE ARE ADDICTED TO THE SPEED AND HURRY.

When talking about this with my friends, all of us admitted we had little rest or sabbath in our lives. We are men who are pursuing God's heart and seeking him daily, but the way of the world has crept in such that we weren't following the 4th commandment. If you need a measuring stick, ask yourself,

"DO I WANT TO KEEP DOING THIS FOR THE NEXT 30 YEARS?"

If you are in a similar place as me, that question makes you tired just thinking about it.

Let me give you an example. It's a long week at work, a tough commute, the kids don't like the pizza I got them for dinner, and I have barely seen or talked to my wife all week as we run to different commitments. All I want is rest so I sit down and binge watch whatever will keep the kids quiet and let me shut off my brain. But do I ever finish and say, "I am refreshed and rejuvenated." No!

ALL I DID WAS MEDICATE MY MEDIOCRITY. I GAVE MYSELF A FIX TO SHUT DOWN MY BRAIN BUT NOT TO HEAL OR BRING JOY TO MY INNER SELF.

We know there is a problem, but how do we address it? Based on the resources I've found, I have started trying a few practices that have helped. I believe these simple practices could be transformational if applied over the long haul. Here they are:

- Silence
- Sabbath (Day of rest and celebration)
- Soul care
- Surrendering control

I promise I wasn't trying for the alliteration. These practices are intertwined and not totally discreet. I have practiced them just a little bit, and I can already see fruit. I will warn you that it will take some effort. These will not come easy. We have been conditioned by the world to be stimulated and busy. But trust me once you taste what is available, you will want it even more.

Here are a few of the other resources I have found helpful:
Fight Hurry, End Hustle Podcast by Jefferson Bethke and John Mark Comer
To Hell With the Hustle by Jefferson Bethke

GOD IS SOVEREIGN

I was watching *The Crown* on Netflix and part of the dialogue gave me some insight into something I have been trying to better understand about God. Margret Thatcher said power is taking action, and the Queen said, as Sovereign, power often means doing nothing. Wow, this is two very different views on power.

One of my frontiers is parenting my six-year-old son. My natural instinct is to parent him by controlling him. Do this, don't do that, etc. This is also how I think about God sometimes. God is in control so he is dictating every little thing. However, it is more true that God is Sovereign.

He created everything and is the ultimate power over everything. As a Sovereign ruler, he does not need to dictate every little thing that happens. Instead, he sits back and does nothing. He lets his creation learn from experience and from his word. He lets them make mistakes so they can grow in maturity. For example if you are hiking and your child is running recklessly along the trail, do you intervene or do you allow the child to fall and scrape their knee and use discipline for training?

HOW DO YOU VIEW GOD? IS HE IN CONTROL OR SOVEREIGN?

FEAR

"There is no fear in love. But perfect love drives out fear, because fear has to do with punishment. The one who fears is not made perfect in love." 1 John 4:18 NIV

Good morning, brothers! There was so much in this verse when I read it this morning. Ultimately, fear is rooted in some level of unbelief.

It makes me think about the martyrs who willingly gave their lives on behalf of the gospel. Think about the certainty in God's promises that would have taken—a certainty that I don't have a lot of the time.

What is it that you fear? Is it losing something, or having something taken away punitively? Is it lack of control over some part of your life? I am praying today that the Spirit helps us all identify and root out those fears and the unbelief that is causing them to continue hanging around.

I am encouraged by the end of this verse because even though we may not have been perfected in love yet, Jesus is still at work and we get the chance to be more and more like him everyday.

WHAT DO YOU FEAR?

WEEK 3.DAY 3
MORNINGS WITH MY BOYS

It's 6 AM. My boys are wide awake, and I'm looking for an excuse to stay in bed. Oftentimes, it's easier for me to go downstairs, throw on Netflix, lay back on the couch, and grab a few extra Zs.

But this summer, with encouragement from my wife, I've tried to be more disciplined with our morning routine. We wake up, head downstairs, play with LEGO, draw, and read library books.

This gives me the opportunity to pick up any clutter left over from last night, which often includes a few Transformers from last night's epic battle. I get the chance to cook my boys a hot breakfast, and then I enjoy eating with them before I head off to work.

During this time, we get to catch up, talk about our goals for the day, and what I expect from them. This is not something new for them; we do the same thing at dinner time, but these meals feel different. It's just me and the boys, eating bacon, and talking about our future. We let mom sleep in a little since she's up most nights with our newest addition.

I'm starting to enjoy these times with my boys. Do they still ask for TV in the morning? Some days. Do I still fight the urge to lay back? Sure. But here's the thing—it's a start.

I'm taking it one day at a time. There's so much more I would like to add to our morning routine. I want to exercise and read the Bible. I want to write, journal, and pray. I want to practice visualization and goal setting.

And I want my boys to be by my side throughout this routine. These are all important activities to set the foundation for their future, and I need them now to be successful today.

I'm working on it, I'm working on our mornings. Are they perfect? Far from it, but we're moving along and we'll get there. I have hope for it.

WHERE DO YOU NEED TO CREATE TIME FOR REAL CONVERSATION WITH THOSE AROUND YOU?

BEING A STRONG DAD

I read from the book *Strong and Kind: Raising Kids of Character* by Korie Robertson today and wanted to share a quote that got me thinking about God's love and discipline.

"Being strong and confident, especially as a dad, does not mean that we should love less or not be soft and tender with our children. Those moments should be more frequent than the stronger moments required for disobedience. But it takes both strong love and strong discipline to create a healthy environment for children."

This is so true about God. He loves us unconditionally and much more than we deserve. That being said, he doesn't shy from correcting us when correction is needed. I pray that I can love more like God and correct in the same way he does, and that would draw those around me closer.

ARE YOU MORE INCLINED TO BE STRONG OR LOVING?

HOW CAN YOU GROW IN BOTH AREAS?

SAFE IS NOT SAFE

I've started training to run ultramarathons and have been listening to audiobooks while out on my long runs. The first on my list is *Developing the Leader Within You* by John C. Maxwell. Maxwell loves poetry and limericks and will often drop a quick one in the middle of the text. I'm really enjoying them. This one stood out to me in the moments I struggled to catch my breath:

> "There was a very cautious man
> Who never laughed or played
> He never risked, he never tried,
> He never sang or prayed.
> And when one day he passed away,
> His insurance was denied,
> For since he never really lived,
> They claimed he never really died."

He never risked, **he** never tried, **he** never sang or prayed. This line continues to echo in my head.

Am I playing it safe when it comes to being a husband? A father? A friend? What areas in my life am I afraid to step into and take those risks? Praying with my sons? Taking true time for God? Being disciplined in my training and seeing true results?

WHERE ARE YOU PLAYING IT SAFE?

DEEP DIVE: SILENCE

Until recently, my days were full of noise. I told myself I was trying to learn, trying to be efficient, and trying to squeeze everything I could out of each day. I would listen to a podcast while commuting, watch the news while I cooked dinner, and listen to music while I ran. All good, right?

I had filled my life to the point that the only time there was silence was when my head hit the pillow. I didn't think twice about this and saw it as a positive until I stumbled on to some teachings that opened my eyes. In *To Hell With the Hustle*, Jefferson Bethke says,

"NOISE IS AN AIRBORNE PATHOGEN WE ARE BREATHING IN CONSTANTLY.... OUR BRAINS ARE LITERALLY EXHAUSTED BECAUSE OF THE NOISE."

That resonated with me, especially after going to an elementary school fundraiser in a gymnasium where the music and kids playing combined into such chaotic noise that my head wanted to explode.

Someone once encouraged me to ask,

"WHAT CULTIVATES YOUR GRATITUDE TOWARDS GOD?"

For me, one answer is spending time in nature, in silence. When I see a beautiful sunrise, I thank God for his goodness. When I go for a run, if I can shut off the podcasts or music, I feel like I can hear God clearly. I feel him stirring my soul. However, none of this happens if my mind is distracted by noise.

I realized I had to create space for God to enter into my day. He is a gentleman. While he can put a blinding light in my path and say, *"Listen up!"* He instead chooses to speak quietly. This is why silence is so important. I need to shut off all the noise and distractions to hear him. The silence also causes discontent in my own soul to stir, which is probably why I have filled the silence with noise for so long.

I HAD TO CREATE SPACE FOR GOD TO ENTER INTO MY DAY.

Ok, don't believe me? Let's give this a try. Open your phone and set a timer for 1 minute. Make sure you are in a relatively quiet place and free of distractions. Sit silently for 1 minute and see what comes to mind.

For me, my inner self comes alive in silence. I think about my day, my emotions, my dreams, and so much more. These are things that get pushed below the surface when I have noise blaring and am running from one thing to the next.

I really like how John Ortberg describes it in *Soul Keeper*. He describes our outer self and inner self. He says your soul integrates your will (intentions), your mind (thoughts and feelings, values and conscience), and your body (face, body language, and actions) into a single life. He notes that we often neglect our inner self (soul) because it is invisible. He says:

"We all have two worlds, an outer world that is visible and public and obvious, and an inner world that may be chaotic and dark or may be gloriously beautiful. In the end, the outer world fades. We are left with the inner world. It is what we will take with us." John Ortberg, *Soul Keeper*

THINK ABOUT THAT. YOUR INNER SELF IS WHAT YOU WILL BE LIVING WITH...FOREVER!

I think it is worth putting some effort into our souls, so let's get to the practical part. You may ask, "Should I just sit here silently?" Yes...but you will probably need some help. This has been a hard practice for me to pick up so I have tried a few things.

First, I have tried to incorporate silence into a few of my routines, like the first few minutes of my commute or when I go for runs.

Second, I have used the *One Minute Pause* app by Wild at Heart. This app is meant to help you stop a few times per day to just reflect. It has amazed me how hard it is to take a one minute or three minute pause in the middle of a normal, chaotic day. When I have done it, it is amazing how God speaks and restores.

Third, I have gone to a cabin in the woods and unplugged for a few days. Now, this is graduate-level silence. In my case, I did this with my men's group, so it wasn't complete isolation. It was a deliberate attempt to unplug and fight back against the attention economy on my phone and computer where companies are fighting and monetizing my attention.

I HAVE HAD TO FIGHT FOR SILENCE, AND IT HAS BEEN WORTH IT BECAUSE IT HAS BEEN THE GATEWAY TO REST/SABBATH, SOUL CARE, AND SURRENDERING CONTROL.

I know I have a long way to go, so I hope you will join me on this journey to develop our inner worlds.

Here are a few of the other resources I have found helpful:
One Minute Pause App by Ransomed Heart
The Spiritual Guide by Michael Molinos

ENCOURAGE AND BUILD UP

"...encourage one another and build each other up..." 1 Thessalonians 4:11 NIV

This verse hit me this morning because, during the last few weeks, the enemy has been sending a lot of attacks towards me around loneliness. I have felt alone as COVID has led to cancelling large gatherings and family visits. It has reduced how much I see my close friends. Also, the day to day part of life being living in my house, instead of out at work, has left me feeling lonely.

Then yesterday, I got to do Sunday Runday with my friend for the first time in six weeks. It was so refreshing because we spent the 10 mile run encouraging and building each other up.

This is what I seek from my brothers in Christ. We need to make sure we are encouraging and building each other up so we can resist the attacks of the enemy and do the work God has called us to.

WHO DO YOU NEED TO ENCOURAGE AND BUILD YOU UP? WHO ENCOURAGES AND BUILDS YOU UP?

TRAIN YOURSELF

I've been engaging my dad a lot more on random topics—just trying to be more intentional about pursuing him. And the other day he sent me a passage he recently came across in his study that he had often walked through with his father back in his teen years:

"Do not waste time arguing over godless ideas and old wives' tales. Instead, train yourself to be godly. "Physical training is good, but training for godliness is much better, promising benefits in this life and in the life to come."" 1 Timothy 4:7-8 NLT

We were made to train for godliness. While the yoke of Jesus is easy, there is also a discipline to sanctification. There is training for it. So while embracing the gospel would lead us away from a "try harder" Christianity, each of us should be actively doing some things to kill sin in ourselves and pursue a greater relationship with Jesus.

HOW ARE YOU TRAINING FOR GODLINESS?

SPENDER OR PLANNER

I was talking with my mom earlier this year about her finances and she said something that really took me back. She said, "I never knew what was going to happen today or this week, so I didn't plan for a future that could so easily be turned upside down."

It took me back a bit because my response to uncertainty is to plan out every detail at the expense of enjoying today. This is an area God has been working on me. God has asked me to allow my wife to make more financial decisions for our family because she can allow herself to spend and give more freely than I can. And I'm slowly learning to plan a little less and live a little more.

On the flip side, my mom is learning to make sacrifices today for the benefit of herself and family over the next 20 to 30 years. This much like what Jesus says in Luke 14:28-30, we should estimate the cost and plan before we get started building.

WHICH DO YOU RESONATE MORE WITH (SPENDER OR PLANNER) AND WHAT HAS GOD SAID TO YOU ABOUT IT?

WEEK 4.DAY 4
LOVE

What do you love? Your family, your kids, your car, a trip to Taco Bell after a long day of work?

We have devalued the word love in our culture. We use the word so often it loses its intensity. For that reason, I want to look today at what the disciple whom Jesus loved says about love.

"This is real love—not that we loved God, but that he loved us and sent his Son as a sacrifice to take away our sins." 1 John 4:10 NLT

That is a pretty high bar. Real love involves **sacrifice.** Serious sacrifice. Think about that. He sent his Son to come and die for us. That is real love. So what should we do?

"Dear friends, since God loved us that much, we surely ought to love each other." 1 John 4:11 NLT

I ~~love~~ (oops) appreciate how John spells it out for us in such simple language and how relevant this message is today.

WHAT DO YOU LOVE?
WHO DO YOU NEED TO LOVE?

YOU WILL REIGN

"And you have caused them to become a Kingdom of priests for our God. And they will reign on the earth." Revelation 5:10 NLT

Really looking at this verse as I read through Revelation, it struck me. I will reign. I will reign on the earth! God will give me a kingdom. Not the Kingdom, but a kingdom. This piece of his Kingdom will be my responsibility...for *eternity!*

You will reign and rule over a piece of the Kingdom of God! Wow! That is pretty amazing. But hey, think about today. God has given a kingdom here to help you prepare for the kingdom you will rain over in eternity. God has put things under your authority. Maybe it is your family or your house. At a bare minimum, God has made you the king of your own body and your own self.

This should give you a different perspective. It should make us step back and think. We are not just living our lives here on Earth to get things, make memories, or give our kids a better life. We are stewarding the Kingdom of God. We are doing what Adam and Eve were created to do: to reign and rule over God's creation. Are we doing it well?

I think modern life removes us from this idea. A friend of mine bought a property of five acres that was rundown. He has been fixing up the house and cleaning up the land. He has been forced to tangibly put his hands on creation and tame it. He is reigning and ruling over it. He has cut down the scraggly trees that are stealing sunlight from the fruit trees.

This is our calling. This is our life's purpose. Just like God created Adam and Eve to reign and rule over the garden, he created us to reign and rule over the new Earth. Our time now is to practice and train, to gain the skills, to gain the knowledge, and to learn to trust in the Father.

WHAT KINGDOM HAS GOD ENTRUSTED YOU WITH?

DEEP DIVE: SABBATH

We have talked about the problem of busyness and how silence is the gatekeeper to finding rest. Now, we are going to talk about Sabbath. I started digging into the idea of Sabbath earlier this year when I realized I knew it was a commandment, but it had no real part in my life. I do my best to follow all the other commandments, but on Sabbath, I had missed the mark. Or more accurately, I hadn't even considered it as a mark I should hit. I heard a few podcasts talking about it and even secular outlets were talking about the value of rest.

FIRST, WE NEEDED TO DEFINE WHAT SABBATH IS FOR OUR FAMILY

You see, my wife and I were on different pages as to what Sabbath is. I think it is quite common that people have different backgrounds and both positive and negative experiences with Sabbath. In *To Hell With the Hustle*, Jefferson Bethke calls it a day of resistance against the production-driven world we live in. He says, "it's about the deep sense of joy and filling and celebration. It's set apart and different. It is the day of rest, but not in the sense of "let's sit there and eat potato chips all day and do nothing.""

BETHKE DESCRIBES SABBATH AS A DAY OF DELIGHT LIKE CHRISTMAS 52 TIMES A YEAR.

Another great teaching on Sabbath comes from Jon Tyson's talk titled *Rest Must Be Stronger Than Exhaustion*. He lays out two key points on Sabbath: resting and feasting. I realized I needed to move away from resting by watching TV and instead rest by ignoring the clock, leaving my phone on the kitchen counter, walking in the neighborhood, or taking a nap. On feasting, Jon Tyson really nails it. He says,

"WE MUST ARRANGE OUR LIVES SO THAT SIN NO LONGER LOOKS GOOD TO US."

As I grew up, it felt like much of Christianity was about what you could not do (no sex, no alcohol, no rock'n roll). I felt like the benefits of following Christ came once we had died and we were all raised to life again. But that is not what the Bible says. We are meant to experience a glimpse of what God has for us in eternity while we are still alive. We are meant to use the Sabbath to celebrate what he has created on the other six days of the week.

SABBATH IS MORE THAN WORSHIPING GOD AND RESTING; WE SHOULD ALSO CELEBRATE THE WORK GOD HAS DONE AND FEAST ON THE BOUNTY OF HIS CREATION.

These great messages have inspired my family to start practicing the Sabbath. I say practice because I have found that it takes a lot of repetition. It is not perfect and magical the first time, but I can see it's working. Practically speaking, we have kept the Sabbath days free of rules or schedule. For example, we don't have a list of what we can and cannot do. We normally start with dinner at night. We have found that eating at our dining room table instead of in the kitchen helps set the meal apart (even when the meal is just takeout). We sleep in as long as our two kids let us. We head to the community workout at our neighborhood gym. Instead of rushing home to get lunch and get our day started, we talk with our friends and let our boys play around. We have lunch and then we might go for a hike, take a nap, or watch a movie depending on how we are feeling. We have found that one of the most freeing things is not having a schedule. We move between activities without the clock looming over us.

One of the things many people suggest is to prepare before the Sabbath so that cleaning the house or grocery shopping don't spoil your day. With that said, I do enjoy grocery shopping when it's for the purpose of making a special meal for family and friends, so that could be part of Sabbath for me if I do it with a restful and joyful heart. This is where Jesus' teaching comes in. He called out the religious of his time because they had made so many rules around the

Sabbath that they missed the point. It is meant to be full of rest and celebration so don't make the mistake of too many rules. One of the simplest takes on it is this:

SIX DAYS A WEEK WE PRODUCE THINGS, AND ONE DAY A WEEK WE ENJOY THE THINGS GOD HAS PROVIDED.

I know I have a long way to go to learn how to Sabbath well, but I am thankful that I have started the journey. Do you want to join in, too?

Here are a few of the other resources I have found helpful:
Rest Must Be Stronger Than Exhaustion Sermon by Jon Tyson
Take the Day Off Sermon by Robert Morris
Fire Your Boss: Discover Work You Love Without Quitting Your Job (Chapter 13 on Play) by Aaron McHugh
The Ruthless Elimination of Hurry by John Mark Comer
Practice the Rule Sermon by Matt Chandler

WEEK 5.DAY 1
WHERE AM I?

Where am I? Sound familiar? All too often, the answer feels like, "Not where I thought I'd be and not happy about it." I'm looking for my circumstances to change and so I'm putting off other things...often good things, things that would be fulfilling or beneficial or just plain fun...until they do. Take a look at this scripture.

"This is what the Lord of Heaven's Armies, the God of Israel, says to all the captives he has exiled to Babylon from Jerusalem: "Build homes, and plan to stay. Plant gardens, and eat the food they produce. Marry and have children. Then find spouses for them so that you may have many grandchildren. Multiply! Do not dwindle away! And work for the peace and prosperity of the city where I sent you into exile. Pray to the Lord for it, for its welfare will determine your welfare."

This is what the Lord of Heaven's Armies, the God of Israel, says: "Do not let your prophets and fortune-tellers who are with you in the land of Babylon trick you. Do not listen to their dreams, because they are telling you lies in my name. I have not sent them," says the Lord.

This is what the Lord says: "You will be in Babylon for seventy years. But then I will come and do for you all the good things I have promised, and I will bring you home again. For I know the plans I have for you," says the Lord. "They are plans for good and not for disaster, to give you a future and a hope. In those days when you pray, I will listen. If you look for me wholeheartedly, you will find me. I will be found by you," says the Lord. "I will end your captivity and restore your fortunes. I will gather you out of the nations where I sent you and will bring you home again to your own land."" Jeremiah 29:4-14 NLT

The Old Testament prophet Jeremiah knows a thing or two about "not where I thought I'd be and not happy about it."

Here's my takeaway this morning: God says, "I'm going to ask you to follow me right where you are for a little bit. Begin focusing on me, not your circumstances."

"Do the things that are good and healthy right where you are…including working for the benefit of the place you currently find yourself no matter how little you think they deserve your best effort."

"I promise you that I'll take care of you. I promise you that I have good things in store for you. You DO NOT have to **earn** them, but you DO need to trust me where you are instead of waiting to trust me, believe in me, or thank me only after your circumstances have changed."

God, help me see where You are right now.

HOW CAN I STAY PRESENT AND LOOK TO THE FUTURE WITH HOPE? WHAT DO YOU WANT ME TO DO TODAY…RIGHT WHERE I AM?

WHERE ARE WE GOING?

Where am I? What's going on? What am I supposed to do? Read Psalm 139:1-6. God says, "You're not really lost...I know exactly where you are, and regardless of the narrative that you think has been written thus far, I'm continuing to both blaze a path for you and guard your back."

I realize I don't have to fake it with him. No matter the confidence or bravado or passivity or indifference that I project to everyone else in my life, he sees me and that is an utter relief.

That means there's at least one person in my life I don't have to hide my true self from. That means there's at least one person in my life I don't have to fake it with or project an exhausting false front.

I can just be me, and that alone is an amazing thing that's almost too good to be true. With God, I can just be...me.

GOD, WOULD YOU SHOW ME HOW YOU SEE ME? WHAT DO YOU LOVE ABOUT ME? WHAT DO YOU SEE WHEN YOU LOOK AT ME?

MORE OF WHO I AM

I've noticed that when I allow myself to begin to be transparent and honest with God...to just be myself instead of deceiving myself into thinking I'm able to hide things from him...I often swing to the other extreme of feeling incredible inadequacy.

"He's God! What could I possibly offer? I'm too _______ (young, old, fat, weak, slow, stupid, unskilled, afraid, unqualified, unknown) to be of any use."

Read Jeremiah 1:4-10. God tells Jeremiah that **what** he is and **who** he is are perfectly suited for the tasks ahead.

So it is for you. So it is for me.

You are not "too" anything. You are **exactly** what's needed. And through this invitation, you will become so much more aware of who you really are.

WHAT LIE HAVE YOU BEEN BELIEVING ABOUT YOURSELF?

WHAT IS THE TRUTH GOD SAYS ABOUT YOU?

WEEK 5.DAY 4
I SURRENDER

I admit it, God...I don't know what to do.

You've thwarted all of my attempts at self-sufficiency.

You've given me dreams so big I cannot achieve them without Your help.

You've exposed fears and beliefs of limitations that could cripple me without Your truth and encouragement.

"Teach me your way, Lord; lead me in a straight path because of my oppressors. Do not turn me over to the desire of my foes, or false witnesses rise up against me, spouting malicious accusations." Psalms 27:11-12 NIV

I need You to teach me. I need You to father me...to both tell me the truth of who I am and the truth of my capabilities.

TEACH ME HOW TO LIVE, LORD. WHERE DO I BEGIN?

ASKING FOR DIRECTIONS

Where do I begin?

I know there's more. I know I can be more. But starting out just feels a little (or a lot) overwhelming. What do I do?

"This is what the Lord says: "Stand at the crossroads and look; ask for the ancient paths, ask where the good way is, and walk in it, and you will find rest for your souls. But you said, 'We will not walk in it.'" Jeremiah 6:16 NIV

Ask. Ask for directions.

There is an ancient path. There is a way things work. There are many that have gone before. I am not the first and I am not alone. I don't have to figure it out for myself however tempting that plan may be.

I am part of a much larger story...one that began long before me and will continue long after...but a story that specifically and uniquely includes ME! And asking after that path and then walking it will bring me rest. I think I'm starting to feel hope.

WHAT IS THE DIRECTION THE FATHER IS ASKING YOU TO GO?

DEEP DIVE: SOUL CARE

"MY SOUL JUST CAN'T DO LIFE AT THE SPEED OF SMARTPHONES." -JOHN ELDREDGE

Now, let's dive into soul care. Go read John Ortberg's book *Soul Keeper*. It is an amazing book on why we need soul care and how to practice it. I don't have anything to add. Devotional done.

That wasn't very soulful, was it? It really is a great book, but I will still give my take on the issue. First, think about how we use the word soul in our culture: soul food, soul music, soul crushing. Part of our culture wants to replace the word soul with self. I even thought about titling this entry "Self Care" to make it sound more appealing. However, your self and soul are not the same thing. Think about it, self music, self food, self crushing? It just isn't the same. Why?

SELF MAKES YOU THINK YOU CAN DO IT YOURSELF, BUT THE SOUL REMINDS US WE WERE CREATED FOR THE CREATOR.

49

Sin damages our souls, but our soul is healed by confessing. Think of the phrase, "It felt so good to get that off my chest." What is the universal truth that people are experiencing? Their souls are being healed by confessing their sin to someone. The opposite is true when we sin because to sin, we often must lie not only to others but also to our inner self.

Ortberg describes the outer and inner self. He says your soul integrates your will, your mind, and your body into a single life. He notes that we often neglect our inner self (soul) because it is invisible, but it holds our thoughts and hopes.

HOW DO YOU HAVE AN INNER SELF THAT IS THRIVING NO MATTER WHAT IS HAPPENING ON THE OUTSIDE?

Well, I think it is helpful to consider what our soul needs, which is depth. Your soul is not surface level. I have found that to even start engaging my soul, I need quiet and to slow down, hence the deep dives on silence and Sabbath before this one. Think about it. If you pause and sit in silence, does your mind go to simple thoughts or does it go to deeper, soul thoughts?

"I am reminded when I'm alone that God loves me—that there is something about life that is infinitely deeper than all of my outer life." John Ortberg, *Soul Keeper*

Here is what else Ortberg says:

    The soul needs a keeper
    The soul needs a center
    The soul needs a future
    The soul needs to be with God
    The soul needs rest
    The soul needs freedom
    The soul needs blessing
    The soul needs satisfaction
    The soul needs gratitude

To summarize these, we need to actively tend to our souls. If you are not actively engaged with your soul, it will be swallowed up by today's culture. John Eldredge talks about how souls were not created to have 1,000+ Facebook friends and to hear about the tragedy and heartache of the whole world every day. Our souls were made to walk with God.

OUR SOUL NEEDS TO DREAM BECAUSE THEY WERE MADE FOR ETERNITY.

The soul has unlimited needs. This is why greed exists and even millionaires are not satisfied with what they have. Our soul's unlimited needs are meant to be satisfied by God's unlimited grace.

As I have pursued soul care, it has been apparent that this is a long process that is fighting against the culture of our day. However, it is well worth it because it is a life-giving practice that is shaping who I will become.

Here are the other resources I have found helpful:
    Soul Keeper by John Ortberg
    Practice the Rule by Matt Chandler
    Get Your Life Back by John Eldredge

WEEK 6.DAY 1
BEAUTY

"He has made everything beautiful in its time. Also, he has put eternity into man's heart, yet so that he cannot find out what God has done from the beginning to the end." Ecclesiastes 3:11 ESV

Why is nature so universally seen as beautiful? Pretty much everyone describes nature's wonders like the Grand Canyon or a great waterfall as beautiful.

Lately, I have been reading Genesis to my sons and Revelation on my own. It is pretty striking how beautiful the garden is described. But I had forgotten that there is also beauty in Revelation.

"Then I saw a new heaven and a new earth, for the old heaven and the old earth had disappeared. And the sea was also gone. And I saw the holy city, the new Jerusalem, coming down from God out of heaven like a bride beautifully dressed for her husband." Revelation 21:1-2

There will be a new heaven, a new earth, and a new Jerusalem, and they will be beautiful. God has designed nature to be beautiful and to call out to us. It is meant to remind us of the beautiful garden of the past and the beauty of the new heavens and earth in the future.

STOP TODAY AND NOTICE BEAUTY

WEEK 6.DAY 2
BATTLE TO BOND

Is it just me or is it hard to have close guy friends as you get older? There are the husbands of my wife's friends, the guys at work, or the neighbor who I wave to in the afternoon, but these are not the close relationships I am looking for.

Our culture has moved to isolate us. Our enemy wants to isolate us. It is easier for him to attack a single warrior than a group of warriors that joined together and are ready to fight.

But how do you do this? How do you find other warriors to join with? I have a mentor who says that men "battle to bond", (women tend to "bond to battle" - more easily forming deep relationships which they then call upon in times of struggle). That seemed like a trendy phrase when I first heard it, but the more I reflected on it, the more I found its truth in my life.

I bonded most with men when we went through a battle together. Since it is not practical for most of us to join the military and go fight a battle just to find fellow warriors, how do I apply that in everyday life? I seek opportunities to battle with other men. This could be a long run, a hike, or a camping trip. It could be an adventure or obstacle race. It could be tackling a home renovation project.

I have learned that I need close male friends, and mine are not found sipping lattes at the local coffee joint, but on cold and muddy trails at 3 AM. Where are yours?

WHO WILL GO INTO BATTLE WITH YOU?

WEEK 6.DAY 3
WHY?

If you have ever had a young child, you've heard the question: Why?

If you have ever taken a financial or job risk, you've heard the question: Why?

If you have ever run an ultramarathon, you've heard the question: Why?

If you are like me, there are surface level answers for all those questions. However, there is also something deeper. For the longest time, I would just give the surface level answer. Something like, I'm taking this risk because I think it'll pay off. I run ultramarathons because I like to compete.

However, when I ask myself, "Why?" If I allow myself to dig deeper, I can really get to the root of things. Let's take ultra running for example. Why do I run ultras? The surface level answer is I like to run.

Now let's go deeper. I like to stay physically fit. I like the challenge of running with other men. I bond with people through running and challenging experiences. I think when we attempt hard things and accomplish them, we mirror God's story and his request for us to sacrifice things for his glory.

I like to run ultramarathons because it pushes me to the point where my body and mind are stripped down, and I have a direct communication line to the Father. It puts me in a place where I no longer talk to him like I'm trying to sound important or spiritual; I just speak directly to him with brutal honesty. In those times when I am weakest, he speaks. It comes in words of scripture, encouragement, or hope. Multiple times when I am in the place that ultra runners call the "pain cave," he meets me there.

Now don't get me wrong here, this is not like the suffering of a martyr. Though, I do believe it's part of the training God has called me to. It is seeking out hard things so that I can remember my own ability is not enough. I must rely on him.

This devotional is not meant to be about ultra running. What I want to get across is that there is value to asking yourself the question "Why?" and to take that question beyond surface level. Why am I doing this? Why do I behave this way? To answer these questions honestly, you might need to really push yourself to your limits to strip down all your ego and personality to really get to the core of it.

So, start asking yourself...

WHY?

WEEK 6.DAY 4
GOD LOVES ME

God loves me. God loves you. Sounds simple, right?

At the beginning of each year, I pray for a word to focus on for the year. I am seeking something that God wants to teach me or knows that I am going to need. Last year, the word was Love. This seemed like one of the most simple messages of the gospel that I should easily have mastered.

However as I reflected on God's love for me, I realized I needed that message to move from head knowledge to heart knowledge. I needed to rest in God's love and not try to earn it or be worthy of it.

I would take a moment to pray and God would say, "Sit and receive my love." I would respond, "Ok, got it. Now what do you want me to *do*?" He would gently respond, "Rest in my love."

His message was impeccably timed as 2020 moved along and COVID hit. I found myself at home having to rest in his love and, amazingly, be at peace with it. You see, the cool thing is that when you listen to the small, still voice, it prepares you for what is to come. It gives you a peace that surpasses all understanding.

HOW DO YOU EXPERIENCE GOD'S LOVE?

WEEK 6.DAY 5
ADVENTURE

I love adventure. But I guess I should define adventure or, even better, tell you about one of my adventures.

In 2019, two of my friends and I set out on a two day land navigation race called The Stockville put on by Rootstock Racing. We covered about 40 miles in the two days finding checkpoints in the woods and mountains with just a map and compass. It was a challenge. It was exhausting. It was an *adventure*.

So why do I seek out adventure? I think my heart is drawn to digging deep and doing things that I am not sure I can do. I mean words can't explain the exhilaration of finding a checkpoint in the woods in the dark.

Also, adventuring has often put me in situations where I recognized how much I need God. The mountains, the weather, and sleep deprivation are all too big for me to control. I need to call out to him to help me get by or dig out the last bit of energy.

PUSH YOURSELF, PLAN AN ADVENTURE FOR YOU AND YOUR FRIENDS.

DEEP DIVE: SURRENDER

"I GIVE EVERYONE AND EVERYTHING TO YOU, LORD; I GIVE YOU EVERYONE AND EVERYTHING."

I first thought about this and started writing before COVID-19 was a thing. But by the time I shared it for the first time, COVID was changing our lives. If you thought you could control the world around you, I would bet the coronavirus crisis is showing you just how much you can't. Schools closed, sports cancelled, churches shut down, people got laid off and stock markets were erratic. All this made it clear, we are not in control.

Jesus says, "Come to me, all you who are weary and burdened, and I will give you rest. Take my yoke upon you and learn from me, for I am gentle and humble in heart, and you will find rest for your souls. For my yoke is easy and my burden is light." Matthew 11:28-30 NIV

HE IS ASKING US TO SURRENDER TO HIM TO RECEIVE REST.

I have found that one of the obstacles for me finding rest is my desire to control things in my life, so let's talk about what I mean by surrender.

Think surrendering control in terms of driving a car. I am driving my car and need to sneeze. I grip the steering wheel tightly with both hands to try to control the car while I sneeze violently. The car jerks sharply to the left almost hitting the car next to me as I try harder to control the steering wheel and my body involuntarily convulses with each sneeze. I feel like that is how I often behave in life. When things come at me, I try to control things more at the exact time I am incapable of controlling them.

Let's try this again. It is the same circumstances: I am driving and need to sneeze. This time I tell the passenger, "I need to sneeze; take the wheel!" I surrender control of the steering wheel to the passenger and sneeze. The car stays in its lane, and all is good. This is what God wants us to do.

HE WANTS US TO RECOGNIZE THAT WE CANNOT CONTROL EVERYTHING AND WE NEED TO SURRENDER CONTROL OF OUR LIVES TO HIM.

In his book *Get Your Life Back*, John Eldredge calls this practice "benevolent detachment." He talks about letting our worries go and giving them over to God. This is about trusting that God will take care of those worries. I often try to control my job, my life, my family, and much more. What is the result of this? Burnout.

The World Health Organization has now classified burnout as a disease. They say it is characterized by feelings of energy depletion or exhaustion, increased mental distance from one's job, or feelings of negativism or cynicism related to one's job and reduced professional efficacy.

I have started the practice of praying, "Lord, I give you everyone and everything." I pray this over my wife and two boys as I leave my house in the morning, and I pray it over my work as I am driving home at night. I have noticed a huge difference. In the past, I would think about work all night. What should I focus on the next day? What could I have added to this or that project? I noticed that once I started to surrender control at the end of each day, I was more able to be at home and be present with family.

WE NEED TO SURRENDER CONTROL TO OUR FATHER AND NOT JUST GIVE CONTROL AWAY TO THE WIND.

If we go back to our example, I could just let go of the steering wheel when I need to sneeze. However, the car will go off course just like if you were trying to control it. I think this is the approach of people who say things like, "what happens, happens." We must recognize that this is releasing control, but instead of giving it over Jesus (who has offered us rest in exchange), we are surrendering control to the world and giving the enemy a strong foothold.

THE PRACTICE OF SURRENDERING CONTROL IS SIMPLE BUT TAKES TIME TO TAKE ROOT.

I found that every day or week or month the surrendering gets deeper. I realize I am still trying to control things that I had thought I had surrendered. That is why, I keep asking the Father what I am trying to control and what do I need to surrender.

Friends, we were not meant to bear the burdens of this world. We were not meant to control our lives. Jesus told us to surrender control to him and we would find rest. We were meant to live life with Christ and rule and reign with him.

WE WERE MADE TO RULE WITH CHRIST.

LET IT BREATHE

Dream big...and then let the dream start breathing.

If you've never seen it, we strongly encourage you to check out the most recent adaptation of "The Secret Life of Walter Mitty." It hits on so many elements that we at Strong Towers are passionate about...not the least of which is transitioning our dreams from mental flights of fancy to solid, achievable reality. Dreams that go from mental escapism to physically, mentally, emotionally, and spiritually challenging and testing our limits.

It's also a beautiful commentary on pursuing the beauty in our lives (both in nature and in the woman who has captured our heart) and overcoming our inclinations toward passivity or over-dominance...but more on that later.

For now, it's the intense illustration of allowing our deeply buried desires to invite us into places of true joy and adventure that we want to focus on.

Check out the film in the next couple days and then check back as we share the segments that have really spoken to us.

Let the dreams come...and then let them begin to breathe.

WHAT ARE YOUR DREAMS?

WEEK 7.DAY 2
CHASED & CAUGHT

Ok, God, I give. Read Psalm 139:7-16

I can't escape You, even if I tried...and that's truly a kindness once I realize it.

You're calling me back (as you did to your people through Jeremiah), and You're drawing me back because You want to be close to me and You want me to want to be close to You. Because when we are, we will see my innermost desires revealed and realized. We will see dreams no longer chased but caught and delighted in...and then new ones formed and we're off on another adventure.

Endless delight and challenge and adventure and delight...forever. That is the life You have made me for and called me to.

WHAT'S MY ANSWER?

WILL I CHASE WITH YOU?

TAKE HEART

Don't lose heart, my friends. After talking about chasing our dreams, I know how quickly frustration and despair can creep in. "It's never going to happen. It's hopeless. Just give up on the dream and settle for the partial and the safe."

Those statements simply aren't true. If you have listened to the Strong Towers podcast, you have heard that our lives haven't been the easiest paths to walk either.

Hope is real. More importantly, hope is internal. It's not something that comes to you. It's something that comes out of you. Here is Proverbs 4:23 from different translations:

"Above all else, guard your heart, for everything you do flows from it." NIV

"Guard your heart above all else, for it determines the course of your life." NLT

"Keep your heart with all vigilance, for from it flow the springs of life." ESV

Your heart is the key to life. It's the key to hope. It's integral to chasing your dreams. Guard it well, my friends...not to lock it up, but to protect it from despair. There is hope.

WHERE DO YOU NEED HOPE?

WEEK 7.DAY 4
I WILL WAIT

"Yet I am confident I will see the Lord's goodness
while I am here in the land of the living.
Wait patiently for the Lord.
Be brave and courageous.
Yes, wait patiently for the Lord." Psalms 27:13-14 NLT

Let this be my prayer, Lord, as I walk with You. As I follow You. As we chase dreams together. I do not need to be afraid...You are with me.

You are so much bigger than and stronger than and smarter than anything or anyone set against me. The best of all the dreams we are chasing is closeness with You...deep connection with You...the kind that allows me to take a deep breath and relax and know that I am safe.

I can wait on You. I don't have to make it happen on my own. I will wait on you. I trust that You love me and that You love the dreams You've placed in me even more than I do.

I will see Your goodness now...in this life...AND in the life to come.

WHERE DO YOU NEED TO WAIT ON THE LORD?

WEEK 7.DAY 5
PRUNING

"He cuts off every branch of mine that doesn't produce fruit, and he prunes the branches that do bear fruit so they will produce even more." John 15:2 NLT

The idea of pruning is worth pondering. If you want better grapes, you need to prune the vines at the end of each year otherwise they won't produce the grapes you want.

This can seem like loss because you are cutting branches from the vine. However, it allows the plant to focus all its energy and nutrients on the branches that produce fruit.

John says the same thing. The Father prunes us so that we will produce more fruit. Pruning is not fun. We will lose things just like the vine loses some branches. If we look backward and focus on what we are losing, we can miss what is coming in the future. Our future is full of even more ripe and beautiful fruit.

There are moments when a small amount of pruning will challenge us to grow towards our full potential, to remove the dead and diseased areas in our lives and bear true fruit.

WHAT AREAS DO YOU NEED TO LET GOD PRUNE SO THAT YOU CAN PRODUCE EVEN MORE FRUIT?

DEEP DIVE: YOU DON'T GO ALONE

This is a follow-up to Let it Breathe on Week 7.Day 1 and may include spoilers from the film "The Secret Life of Walter Mitty."

YOU DON'T ACTUALLY GO IT ALONE.

One of the great icons of American masculinity is the image of the "lone wolf." The man who needs no one and nothing, save for his wits, his rugged good looks, and the occasional female dalliance, and who always wins at the end of the story.

Frontiersmen. Jason Bourne. John Wayne. James Bond (who's British, but whatever).

As I watch *The Secret Life of Walter Mitty*, I'm struck by just how easy it is to buy into this narrative again if I'm not paying attention.

A CURSORY GLANCE SEEMS TO SHOW THE CLASSIC MALE STORY ARC.

One man sets out alone in search of adventure...in search of finding himself...and does...and returns home changed to win the girl and tell off the a-holes in his life...and win.

Except he doesn't.

Without Sean O'Connell's spiritual intervention from the photograph on the wall, Walter never leaves his safe, passive, soul-crushing small story to enter into a larger one.

Without Ted from e-Harmony, Walter never has the companion that witnesses his life from pre-transformation to redeemed and restored new man and who can marvel with him at the change.

Without the introduction of Cheryl's son, Walter never gets to reawaken his inner child...the part of him, even as a grown man, that is still in desperate need of play and adventure.

Without the helicopter pilot, the fighter within Walter continues to lie dormant.

Without the Icelandic hotel keeper, Walter's dead in a volcano eruption.

And let us not forget the woman...

Without Cheryl, Walter is never inspired to play the true man. Without Cheryl, Walter never pieces together the clues of his adventure. Without Cheryl, Walter never leaves the bar in Greenland to leap onto a helicopter. Without Cheryl, Walter doesn't process the pain of his youth and the death of his father.

As John Eldredge says in *Wild at Heart,* every man aches for three things:

1. AN ADVENTURE TO LIVE
2. A BATTLE TO FIGHT
3. A BEAUTY TO FIGHT FOR

And none of those things happen alone. As we are finishing up this devotional and this book, are you still battling alone? Have you found your group of like-minded warriors? If you are still fighting alone, now is the time to take a risk and find some other men to live life with. It might take some trial and error, but remember that all great stories of adventure have ups and downs. The question is how does the main character handle them. In this great adventure, you are the main character. So...

GOD, WHO WOULD YOU HAVE ME INVITE TO JOIN IN THIS JOURNEY?

WHAT ADVENTURE HAVE YOU CALLED ME TO LIVE? WHO AM I MEANT TO LIVE IT WITH?

WHAT BATTLE DID YOU SPECIFICALLY POSITION AND GIFT ME TO FIGHT? WITH WHOM CAN I SHARE THIS BATTLE?

HOW CAN I BETTER FIGHT FOR THE BEAUTY IN MY LIFE? OR HOW CAN I BETTER PREPARE TO FIGHT FOR THE BEAUTY YOU HAVE IN STORE FOR ME ?

EPILOGUE

Thank you for joining us on this journey! We are all on different paths, but we believe we are made stronger when being challenged by others and seeking the wisdom of fellow travelers. God has much more in store for you. We would love to hear from you about how you used this book and about what God has done inside of you.

You can connect with the Strong Towers crew at www.strong-towers.com or search your favorite podcasting app to hear more from our discussions.

We pray that God works inside of you and stirs your heart to pursue him even more. We pray that this is just the beginning of our journey together as we seek to Build Up and Become Strong.

We love you, brothers!